My Savings JAR

Ylanda T. Wilhite

Copyright

Acknowledgement

I would like to thank everyone who provided me with feedback and input for this book. I truly appreciate you for helping me turn the dream of writing a book into reality.

TABLE OF CONTENTS

IT'S MY BIRTHDAY

SCHOOL

The last bell rang for the end of the school week for Chaya and Savanna. Chaya couldn't contain her excitement because the next day was her birthday party. As Chaya and Savanna walked home from school, it was all they could talk about. "You must be super excited about your birthday party tomorrow," Savanna said. "I'm thrilled! I hope you're still able to come. I asked my mom to make strawberry shortcake because it's my favorite. We will also have vanilla ice cream and all of my favorite foods. It's going to be good!" Chaya said.

"I'm so there!" Savanna said excitedly.
"What about presents? Did you ask for anything special?" Savanna asked.
"I asked for a cell phone, but my parents don't want to get one because they think I'm too young. I hope they'll change their minds and surprise me. My second choice would be a jewelry kit to make jewelry. I saw a lady making jewelry on TV, and it looked so cool! I love jewelry with beads best. I'm glad that you're coming. I invited other kids from school and church," Chaya said.

Early Saturday morning, Chaya was awakened by her mom and dad screaming,

"HAPPY BIRTHDAY!

HAPPY BIRTHDAY!

No sleeping in today; it is your big day! The forecast shows no rain, so your birthday party will be outside," her mom said.

Today is off to a great start, thought Chaya. By three o'clock, all the kids had arrived. They were in the yard playing games, listening to music, and eating hot dogs and burgers cooked on the grill.

"Everyone, it's time to sing Happy Birthday to Chaya," her mom yelled.

So everyone started singing the happy birthday song cheerfully.

I'm so excited, and I feel like I'm going to bust open. I'M WINNING! Chaya thought to herself.

"Mom, can I open my gifts now?" Chaya asked.

"Sure, Honey," Chaya's mom replied.

There were two boxes and a few envelopes. All the kids' eyes were focused on Chaya as she opened her gifts. She started with the boxes first. The first box had a lot of wrapping paper and a bow. Chaya ripped the paper apart and tore the box open.

It was full of clothes.

"Honey, I figured you needed some new clothes. I hope you like them," her mom said.

"Thanks Mom and Dad," Chaya said appreciatively.

Clothes are fine, but I was still hoping for a cell phone, Chaya thought disappointedly.

Then, she started to open the next box. She knew it was probably not a cell phone. She ripped the paper off as everyone looked on, revealing a clear box with beads, string, and other things to make jewelry.

"Thank you! Thank you. This is exactly what I wanted," Chaya said excitedly.

Finally, she started opening the envelopes.

Chaya

"Chaya, these are the cards your friends brought you for your birthday. Make sure that you read them and thank everyone," instructed Mom. Chaya started opening the cards, and each one had money in it. She handed the money to her mom as she read each card.

"Although this is your money, I want you to start saving some of the money you get for your birthdays and other occasions. Learning how to save and put money aside for future use is so important." I will give you this jar to start putting your money in. It will be called CHAYA'S SAVINGS JAR." Mom hurried to explain.

As all the kids were looking on and listening to Chaya's mom, Chaya excitedly cut in, "Mom, I hear you. Can we just cut the cake now?"

"Alright, but we will talk more about this later," Mom replied. After Chaya made her wish, her mom then cut slices of cake.

Chaya

Later that night, as Chaya reflected on what a great day and birthday celebration she had earlier, her mom entered her room. "Chaya, your dad and I hope you enjoyed your birthday party; your friends appeared to have had a good time!" Here is the jar that I talked about earlier. I want you to start saving your money. In big print, it had CHAYA'S SAVINGS JAR. You can start with the $75 you received today. You can take $25 to buy whatever you want; the other $50 will go into your savings jar. The goal is to fill the jar up with bills and coins. Once it is full, we will count it together to see how much you have saved. You can use one-half of the savings for something special." Mom explained.

"Like a cell phone?" Chaya eagerly asked.
Mom replied," Your father and I will have to discuss that. You must present your case for why you need a cell phone. I said NEED as opposed to WANT."
"Aren't they the same?" Chaya commented.
"No, NEED is something that you can't live without, and WANT is something you can live without but choose not to," Chaya's mom explained.
"Mom, if I get a cell phone, you can always know where I am. Also, Dad and you do not have to worry because there is no internet or social media. I can just call, text, and play games," Chaya said convincingly.

Chaya

While in bed, Chaya thought about what her mom said. The savings jar was on the nightstand next to her bed. The amount in the jar from her birthday gifts was $50. There were a lot of different bills like $5s, $10s, and some $1s. *I will fill that jar with so much money that the top will not fit. I will save now to have the money for the cell phone later this year,* she thought as she drifted off to sleep.

LEMONADE STAND

soup
soup

During the school lunch break, Chaya and Savanna sat talking. "What a fun birthday party! It is cool that you get to put money into a jar and save it. The money will be all yours! I will ask my mom for a jar to save money, too. Mine will be SAVANNA'S SAVINGS JAR," Savanna said with a grin.

"We should think of ways to make money together and split it between us. Your birthday is in a few months, so you can start saving that money like me," Chaya said.

"I'm not having a party, but I will get money from my grandparents," Savanna said.

"How about a lemonade stand? I saw one in a movie once, and the kids sold cups of lemonade."

"Lemonade?" Savanna asked.

"Yes. Their moms helped make the lemonade and bought the plastic cups. The kids made a sign, and they did the selling. The moms sat outside with them, but they did the work. We can ask our moms if we can sell lemonade and if they will help us!" Chaya suggested.

"Wow, Chaya, that is a good idea! We will make a lot of money to add to our jars. We can do it one Saturday afternoon in front of your house. Your house is near the corner with more cars and people passing by," Savanna added.

“You talk to your mom, and I will talk to mine. This is so exciting! I will talk to you tomorrow,” Chaya said as the lunch break was over.

As soon as Savanna saw Chaya at school the next day, she said, "My mom said she would help us with a lemonade stand. She's excited that you and I want to do this."

"Awesome! My mom said yes, too! She said that she would help us make the lemonade and set it up in my front yard. Savanna, ask your mom to call my mom so they can pick a weekend to do it. We need to make a sign. How much should we charge for a cup of lemonade?" Chaya asked.

“I don’t know, $1?” Savanna suggested.

"Yeah, we can charge $1 and give each person one cookie. That sounds like a good idea; hopefully, our moms will buy everything. This is going to be fun! By the way, did you get a savings jar?" Chaya asked.

"Yes, I got it! I'm going to decorate my savings jar. I told my mom you started with $50 from your birthday gifts. When I woke up this morning, there was $10 in my jar. She said that will help me get started," said Savanna.

"Your mom is so cool," Chaya responded with a smile.

Savanna

A few weeks passed, and it was finally time for the lemonade sale. "Savanna, I'm so glad your mom let you stay over last night. We can start early with making the lemonade and setting everything up," Chaya said.

"This will be epic! All the kids at school will hear about this and be super jealous. Everyone in our class will want to start a savings jar. After our summer break, we can see who saved the most. It can be a contest!" Savanna said.

Fresh homemade lemonade
and one cookie for only $1!
Don t be thirsty or hot;
get a cup of lemonade

"Chaya and Savanna, both of you did a great job on the sign!" Chaya's mom exclaimed, giving the girls a thumbs-up. Savanna loudly read the sign, "Fresh homemade lemonade and one cookie for only $1! Don't be thirsty or hot; get a cup of lemonade today!"

LEMONADE
Fresh homemade lemonade
and one cookie for only $1!
Don t be thirsty or hot;
get a cup of lemonade
today!

As they stood outside behind the table, people started lining up. “How many cups would you like?” Chaya asked.

Savanna and Chaya poured the lemonade and handed out the cookies. The moms took the money and gave change when necessary. Two hours later, they had sold all the pitchers of lemonade and cookies.

"Mom, we sold everything," said Chaya.

"Yes, you did! We are so proud of you, girls! Let's clean up everything, and then you can count your money inside the house," said Savanna's mom.

Savanna and Chaya started taking down the sign and grabbing the garbage to take inside the house. Once inside, Chaya and Savanna poured all the money from the pouch onto the kitchen table. There were a lot of dollar bills and some coins as well.

Savanna
Chaya

"You both count the money first, and then we will count it after you to ensure we count the same amount," Chaya's mom said.

After they counted and their moms confirmed, they had $72.

"Wow! We made $72 in just a couple of hours. That is a lot of money. We should do this every week," Chaya said.

"Slow down, honey. You guys did great and worked hard. We are so proud of both of you. Now, before the two of you split your profits, you have to give us back the money we spent buying the lemons, sugar, cookies, cups, and napkins," Savanna's mom said.

"How much is that?" Savanna asked curiously.

"Well, here's the receipt. The total cost was $20."

"So we have to give that back to you?" Chaya asked.

"Absolutely! Your actual profit is the money you make after removing the cost of buying the materials. That means that Savanna and you will split $52. That is still very good for two hours of work.

We are incredibly proud of the two of you," Savanna's mom replied. Savanna and Chaya looked at each other and started jumping and screaming. They each had $26 to put in their savings jar. Adding that money plus the change Chaya found since her birthday, her savings jar was halfway full. As she went to sleep that night, all Chaya could think of was how close she was to her goal. She also thought about other ways to earn money to add to her jar.

EXTRA CREDIT

Hey, Mom, I finished cleaning up my room and put my clothes in the drawer. Now, can I go over to Savanna's house?" Chaya asked.

"I will have to see; I still have to wash my car," her Mom said.

"In that case, can I earn an extra allowance by helping you clean the car? I can clean out the inside before you start washing the outside," Chaya said.

"So you want me to pay you to help me wash the car?" her mom asked.

"Mom, if I can make money by doing extra chores, my jar will be full sooner. Then, hopefully, Dad and you will let me get a phone. I'm not just asking for money without doing anything. I'm willing to work for it,"

Chaya replied. "Mom, for just $10, I will clean the inside of your car and help wash it. That is a great deal!"

"Okay, Chaya. You have a deal this time! Grab a plastic bag from the cabinet and put all the stuff on the car floor into the bag," her mom replied.

"Awesome! I will do a good job, Mom!" Chaya exclaimed.

After an hour of scrubbing and wiping the car, they were done. "Wow! The car is so clean, it looks almost new. We make a great team!" Chaya yelled.

"Yes, it looks nice. You did an excellent job cleaning the inside, too!

Chaya

Here is your $10 in all single dollar bills.
How many singles equal ten dollars?" her mom asked.
"That is easy; there should be ten single dollar bills.
Thank you, Mom," Chaya said.
"I appreciate your help, and again, you did a really good job! You have really embraced and are working hard to add to your saving jar. That determination and dedication will help you in school and other parts of your life," her mom encouraged her.

"I will put the money in my jar. Mom, can I still go over to Savanna's?" Chaya asked.

Her mom looked at her watch and said, "Yes, but call and check with Savanna's mom first."

"Thanks, Mom! Putting the lid on my jar with this money from chores will be hard. I just might need a bigger savings jar," Chaya said excitedly.

THE COUNT

Chaya

It seems like such a long time since my birthday. Now, here I am six months later, and MY JAR IS FULL! As I sit on the bed looking at my savings jar, I wonder how much money it contains. I can see a bunch of single dollar bills, ten dollar bills, a couple of twenty dollar bills, and many coins like dimes, quarters, and nickels.

If I had to guess, I should have about $100 or a little more. Grandma secretly added a few dollars when she stopped by to visit. Everyone knew I was trying to fill my savings jar, and they all tried to help. I can't wait until Mom gets home from work so she can help me count. After all, she is the one who got me started. Once I count the money tonight, I will start all over again. I might get a bigger jar the next time around. This savings thing is fun! As Chaya was thinking to herself, she heard the front door close. *Time to count,* she thought.

After her mom got home and relaxed, she asked Chaya, "Are you ready? Maybe call to see if Savanna wants to come over and count her savings, too."

"Savanna's jar is not full yet. Should I just pour the money onto the bed?" Chaya said.

"Yes, maybe separate all the bills that look alike and stack all the same coins together. This will make it easier to count and keep track. Once you are done counting, I will count to ensure we come up with the same amount, just like we did after the lemonade sale. There is nothing like saving money to buy what you want or to save it for a rainy day," her mom responded. Chaya looked confused and said, "Why do I need to save money for a rainy day?"

"It is a figure of speech, honey. It means saving money for an emergency," her mom explained.

"Okay, I got it. Look at all the money that is all over the bed," Chaya said, pointing to the bed.

Chaya

“You start to count while I finish dinner. When you are done, just let me know,” said Mom. Chaya started counting, ”I got $135! I'm rich!" Chaya exclaimed with glee. *The cell phone I want is only $120, and Dad promised to give me half the cost. That means he will give me $60, and then I will only have to use $60 of my savings. If Mom and Dad get me the phone, they will just add my phone to their plan.* She thought, *I still have to convince them that I don’t just want a phone but I need it too.*

“Mom, I’m done. I counted $135!" Chaya shouted. "Just give me a few seconds to put this sauce on the spaghetti," her mom replied.

Chaya could barely hold her excitement and said, “Mom, come on! What time will Dad get home? Will he want to go to the mall tonight to see about phones?"

Seeing Chaya's excitement, her mom said, "First, I need you to relax and breathe. Second, your dad is proud of you for setting and meeting your goal, but he’s not going to the mall tonight. Your dad and I have not decided yet about the cell phone. Just give me a few minutes of quiet and no movement while I count.”

When her mom was done counting, she said, “I counted $135 as well. Congratulations!”

Chaya felt like her heart was going to burst open; it was beating so fast! She picked up the phone and called Savanna. “I have $135! I have $135!” she squealed with delight, “I can’t wait until your jar is full, too. We are so lucky!”

GROWING SAVINGS

$
BANK

"Chaya, I don't want you to stop saving now that you have reached your goal. Saving is something that you will do your whole life. If your father and I allow you to get a cell phone, you will have about $75 left in your jar. I want you to continue to save and turn that $75 back into $135, then $200, and so on. However, we must decide what to do with the money you saved. It can't just remain in a jar," her mom said.

"What should I do with it?" Chaya asked.

"We will start by going to the bank and opening your savings account. When you keep your money in a savings account, the bank will pay you money for keeping it in the account. This payment is called interest," her mom explained.

“Why would they do that?" Chaya asked.

“Good question!” her mom said. “The bank uses the money to help companies and people who need it for different projects. The money that the bank gives to them is called a loan. They have to pay back the loan with interest."

Chaya then asked, "What happens if the bank gives the money to someone and they don’t pay it back? Do I lose my money?"

"Again, great questions, honey! The answer is no, you will not lose your money. Your money will always be available to you whenever you want it. All the money in savings accounts is protected by something called insurance, so you don’t have to worry. Dad and I have accounts at the bank, and we have had them for a long time."

Chaya

Mom, I want to put my money in the bank to get paid interest. Can we go tomorrow?" Chaya asked.

"Yes, we can. This is the first step in growing your money. The next step is called investing. I will teach you more about this later. For now, we will open a bank savings account to keep your money safe and earn you interest. In the meantime, I will teach you more ways to grow your savings," her mom explained.

"I will tell Savanna about the savings account and interest. Once she has reached her goal, she can open one too!" Chaya said.

Her mom looked at Chaya and said, "I'm so glad you set a goal, stuck with it, and will continue to build on it. Your dad and I will take you to pick out a cell phone. You have earned it!"

"Thank you so much! I love you." *I can't wait to get a bigger jar to start saving again! Now, I want to save over $200. I will use my jewelry kit to make and sell bracelets at school. I can do it!* Thought Chaya.

The End

Glossary-Words Definition

GLOSSARY- WORDS DEFINITION

Insurance: Protection provided to reduce, replace, or prevent the loss of money or something else

Interest: The extra money earned on your savings. Also, the money paid when money is borrowed or loaned to a person or company

Investing: Putting money or time into something that is expected to grow or develop

Loan: Let someone use something that belongs to you, and it is returned later

Need: Something that is hard to live without

Profit: The money made from the sale of something or service after the cost of materials is subtracted

Rainy Day: Saving for a future event or emergency

Savings: Keeping money instead of spending it

Savings Account: A bank account to keep money in

Want: Something a person desires but can live without

Made in the USA
Monee, IL
13 August 2024

63260773R00040